Hermann Josef Weidinger

BLESSED
JAMES KERN
The Priest of Atonement

Translated by Hubert S. Szanto

**Revised Edition 2003
St. Michael's Abbey
Silverado, CA**

First published in Austria in 1960 under the title
Sühnepriester Jakob Kern by Verlag Styria Graz, Vienna

First English Edition 1998
Revised English Edition 2003

Published by
St. Michael's Abbey
19292 El Toro Road
Silverado, CA 92676

Printed by
Image Realm
6627 McKinley Avenue
Los Angeles, CA 90001

Text translated and printed with the permission of
Hermann Josef Weidinger

Photos reproduced with the permission of
Hermann Josef Weidinger
and the Abbey of Geras, Austria

Library of Congress Control Number: 2003107388

ISBN 0-9742298-0-6

Table of Contents

A Letter from the Abbot of St. Michael's Norbertine Abbey

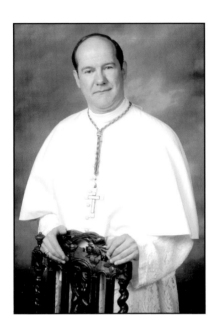

June 6, 2003
Feast of St. Norbert

Dear Readers,

The spirit of St. Norbert given to his followers down through the ages has produced numerous men and women of extraordinary holiness of life. One of these, James Francis Kern, a man of our own time, is the most recent in that line which goes back to the Founder of the Norbertine Order himself. Like St. Norbert, James Kern was a churchman. With the same spirit that enabled St. Norbert to reform the Church of the twelfth century, James directed his efforts to repair the damage done to the Church of the early twentieth century.

In his offering of self as a means of atonement for the failings of a brother priest, Blessed James Kern underlines for the faithful at the beginning of the twenty-first century the importance of the unity of believers in the bond of charity. His life is also a timely reminder of the importance of priestly fidelity, and of the need for all the faithful to support their priests through prayer, penance, and encouragement.

It is my hope and prayer that many will read the life of this young priest who in a few short years of priesthood contributed so much to the building up of Christ's Body here on earth. I wish to thank Fr. Hubert S. Szanto, O.Praem., of St. Michael's Abbey for his translation of this work from the original German.

May all who read this work be inspired to seek God's will without fear and to answer His call regardless of the cost.

Sincerely in Christ and St. Norbert,

+Eugene J. Hayes, O.Praem.
Abbot of St. Michael's Abbey
Silverado, California

Preface to the 2003 Edition

The beatification of Father James Francis Kern by Pope John Paul II on June 21, 1998, was a sign of hope for God's pilgrim people on earth. This simple priest who accepted suffering in a spirit of humble reparation calls humanity back to gospel values that have all but disappeared from the lifestyle of many Christians today. In a particular manner, Blessed James' keen sorrow over the loss of a single priestly vocation in his own day invites us to offer humble reparation in the face of widespread similar losses in our time.

James Kern's thirst to be a priest, his ardent desire for priestly holiness, and his profound love for the gift of the priesthood evoke the beginnings of the Norbertine Order to which he belonged. It was St. Norbert of Xanten, establishing this ancient religious order in the year 1120, who distinguished himself as a champion of priestly holiness in the Gregorian reform movement of the twelfth century. St. Norbert was convinced that through lives of penitent holiness his priests could lift the priesthood from the depths to which it had generally fallen in his time. The rapid expansion of the order across Europe in the twelfth century contributed substantially to the phenomenon which some historians have since dubbed "the exaltation of the priesthood."

Blessed James once wrote, "The priest must be consumed by his vocation. In our days, more than ever, we need devoted and holy priests." The beatification of Father James Kern is therefore a call to priests everywhere to renewal and the pursuit of holiness. It is a call to the faithful to foster priestly vocations through prayer, example, and works of penance and reparation. It is not enough merely to be concerned about the "crisis" in priestly vocations. This "crisis" can only be overcome through a combination of prayer and penance in the life of both priests and laity.

This booklet is a loose translation of the original German work *Sühnepriester: Jakob Kern* by Rev. Hermann Josef Weidinger, O.Praem., published in 1960 by *Verlag Styria Graz* in Austria. Rev. Hubert S. Szanto, O.Praem., Ph.D., of St. Michael's Norbertine Abbey in Silverado, California, translated the book. Several sections of the original work without any direct connection to the life of Blessed

James have been omitted and/or condensed in the English. The German name "*Jakob*" has been rendered by the more familiar English equivalent "James." The first edition was printed in 1998. Rev. Norbert Wood, O.Praem., did the final editing of the 2003 edition and added the new Epilogue and appendices. He was assisted by Rev. Charles Willingham, O.Praem., and frater Ambrose Criste, O.Praem..

Rev. Hubert S. Szanto, O.Praem., Ph.D.
Translator

Chapter 1
The Lord Needs Sacrificial Souls

The pilgrim traveling by rail to visit the tomb of Blessed James Kern is aware of the train's laborious ascent on the last hill of the Manhartsberg where it joins the mountains of the Thaya valley along the southern border of the Czech Republic. Traveling close to what was formerly known as the "Iron Curtain," the small country train reaches a wide bend and approaches Geras-Kottaun, one of the last stations along the way. The green wall of forest respectfully retreats to reveal the ancient abbey of Geras nestled in a forested cove.

Immediately the Norbertine abbey appeals to the eye with its prominent church. Its slender steeple, like a warning finger of God, points to the heavens where clouds and sunshine compete for control: an image of daily life with its constant mixture of somber and bright moments. Meanwhile cars on the Horn-Drosendorf highway rush past the venerable old buildings. The different wings of the baroque monastery cling to the church like trusting children, and the gardens and fishponds behind it are peacefully inviting. On the abbey grounds, in a simple memorial chapel, rest the mortal remains of Blessed James, a Norbertine canon and former resident of this monastery.

In every age the Lord needs sacrificial souls to be instruments of conversion and transformation. Father James was just such a man. He took his vocation as a *canon regular*, which combined the priestly and monastic life in one, very seriously. He offered himself totally, pouring himself out in sacrifice for the benefit of others, literally becoming a priest of atonement, a paschal lamb in the image of Christ crucified.

No one is born a saint. Saints are made by continually striving for the grace of God and allowing it to transform their hearts. This little book will modestly attempt to relate the intense and abundantly fruitful life of Blessed James. His was a life which demonstrates that everything worthwhile and noble in this world requires hard work, daily sacrifice, and great love.

Chapter 2
A Mother's Promise

A baby boy was born to Francis and Anna Kern on April 11, 1897, in the 13th district of Vienna, Austria, at 56 Breitenseerstrasse. The child was baptized "Francis Alexander," after his father and his godfather, Alexander Kern. His father was a professional gardener from Vienna who nevertheless worked at the Viennese ice skating club as a night-porter during this period. Anna was from Landegg near Baden in Lower Austria. Both parents were devout and faithful Catholics, but it was especially Anna who instilled in her son a great trust in God, an unshakeable faith, and a deep piety.

Before the birth of her son Anna Kern's thoughts turned often to the child growing in her womb, the fruit of marital love. In these days of anxious expectation, a desire grew in her heart to make a pilgrimage to a Marian shrine to seek the Virgin Mother's blessing, protection, and intercession for her baby. She went to Maria-Enzersdorf and knelt before the shrine in prayer as only an expectant mother can pray, remaining there for a long time, filled with trust and faith in God. It was at this time that she made a promise: should the baby be a boy, she would entrust him to the Blessed Mother in the hope that she would implore her Son Jesus to call the boy to the priesthood. Anna promised for her part to educate the child in piety and instill in his heart a profound respect and love for the priestly calling.

This prayerful promise was made by a Christian mother who knew that God's help begins where human abilities end. Anna would depart from this life before seeing her prayer answered in the ordination of her son to the priesthood, although she did live to see him enter the seminary. On her deathbed in 1919 she happily told her son about her promise at Maria-Enzersdorf and thanked God that it was soon to be fulfilled. Francis Kern was truly blessed to be the son of such a mother.

Chapter 3
Early Childhood

Francis spent the early years of his childhood at home with his family. He was naturally subject to the same childish faults as other children. At age two he once asked his busy mother where his sister was. She answered abruptly, "In the church." The next thing she knew, her son had disappeared and was nowhere to be found in the house. Rushing into the street she saw him gleefully gazing at the fascinating objects in a store window which had distracted him on the way to look for his sister. As his mother approached, he turned and said innocently, "Look mommy!" The relieved mother gathered him up into her arms, carried him home, and corrected him accordingly.

There were two golden threads present at the beginning of his life which continued to the end: his childlike joy in the Divine Liturgy and his love of prayer. He and his mother, a good teacher of prayer, attended Mass together during the week. This had its effect. One Christmas when he was about four or five he received a train set and a toy horse. When his mother asked him if he was happy with the gifts, little Francis sadly shook his head and said no. His surprised mother asked him the reason, and he responded that he had really wanted "an altar with candlesticks and candles and flowers." He received a play altar shortly thereafter and was overjoyed.

Also about this time there was an incident which shows how his youthful piety was united to a sober common sense. A friend of his, Aloysius Benesch, injured his ankle through carelessness. Little Francis reproached him saying, "Be careful. Your Guardian Angel can't always keep you out of harm's way." When the condition of Aloysius' foot grew worse and the doctors declared that it would have to be amputated, little Francis lingered so long in church praying for him that his parents grew worried over his late return home. But to the astonishment of Aloysius' doctors the foot healed so completely that he was later even cleared for active military service.

Chapter 4
The Call of the Lord

Francis made his first confession in the third grade and received his first Holy Communion in the fourth. During these years he would kneel at his small altar for long periods of prayer and was already freely making sacrifices for the love of God. At age eleven, in 1908, he was confirmed on the feast of Pentecost. He received this sacrament with such devotion that his sponsor was moved to tears at the sight. His classmates also noticed his piety and, not able to understand, they often made fun of him. Francis bore this patiently and even persuaded several of them to join him on occasional visits to church.

The pious little Francis was also a bright student who excelled in school. It became increasingly clear, especially to his good mother, that God had given him the necessary talents to be a priest. It therefore came as no surprise when he entered the junior seminary in Hollabrunn and studied at the public *gymnasium* (the college preparatory liberal arts school from the fifth through the twelfth grade).

A new chapter in his life began with his entrance into the seminary in September of 1908, at age eleven. He loved this time in the junior seminary and often talked about it in later years with face aglow. Since the seminary had its own chapel, Francis and the Savior now lived under the same roof. The young seminarian was frequently drawn to the chapel where he often found himself the only person spending time with the Lord. Francis' perseverance and commitment to his encounters with the Lord developed into the grace of profound prayer, a special gift given to devout and faithful souls.

Francis had a strong devotion to the Sacred Heart of Jesus and the Blessed Virgin Mary. He prayed the rosary daily and began to recite the *Little Office of the Blessed Virgin* when he entered the upper grades at the *gymnasium*. He received Jesus in Holy Communion every day as the Bridegroom of his soul, and grew strong in the life of prayer and virtue. During his personal prayer before the tabernacle, Francis came to understand that real love expresses itself in

renunciation and sacrifice. With the seed of sacrifice thus planted, it only took time to grow into the concept of atonement. This took concrete form in the offering of his body to the Lord through a vow of virginity at age fourteen. Because of his young age, his spiritual director only permitted him to make a temporary vow for one year. A year later, shortly after his fifteenth birthday, he received permission to make the vow for life on April 21, 1912. Francis also joined the Third Order Franciscans at this time in order to imitate the poverty and self-denial of his baptismal patron, Saint Francis of Assisi.

Francis' sincere faith and piety led him to fulfill his obligations conscientiously and directed everything he did. Just as an abundance of underground water pushes up into a natural spring, providing clear, fresh water, the joy and happiness of his pure heart overflowed in his daily life. Francis was one of the happiest young men among his peers. His sense of humor was a positive reflection of his sunny, childlike soul. He was never boring or downcast, and he hardly ever missed a joke or jest, often having the funniest and craziest ideas himself. At the same time he took great care not to insult or hurt anyone.

Francis' love for praying in church grew with time. During times of communal prayer, he loved to use the God-given gift of his clear, ringing voice to sing and pray. On account of his great love for the Mass and Christ's Eucharistic presence, his favorite job in the seminary was to work as sacristan and take care of all the vessels and vestments and the decoration of the altar and chapel. In a nutshell, he was a young man who loved God's house and became an intimate friend of Jesus. This love governed his whole life and never deteriorated into superficial sentimentality. Francis' joyful love expressed itself in genuine kindness and a special horror of doing others harm.

Francis could have ended up like so many others, living an insignificant or mediocre life. But when Christ's call reached his expansive, glowing heart, he responded generously to the call of his Divine Master. The Lord called into the streets and neighborhoods of Vienna, into the crowds and confusion, and this little boy responded. He left father and mother and trustingly followed the call to become Francis Alexander Kern the seminarian.

Chapter 5
The Call of the Emperor

At this time there was a monumental disturbance in the world's political sphere. The vast Austro-Hungarian empire creaked and groaned at its foundations, threatening to collapse. It was clear, despite its show of strength and grandeur, that it was in imminent danger of dissolution. In Sarajevo the first shots thundered, setting off a world war. In Vienna only one thought held the minds of men: to fight for the emperor and the fatherland.

Francis was filled with patriotic zeal and reported for military duty on October 15, 1915, with the 59th infantry in Salzburg. He was eighteen. In January he was transferred to southern Austria, and on May 15, 1916, he was sent to the southern border to fight on the Italian front. With only a few days to say good-bye before facing the prospect of death on the battlefield, he left home a day early in order to keep a prior commitment to make a holy hour in the chapel of Vöcklabruck. He arrived in Schlunders at 1:30 a.m. and got a short night's sleep before rising to find the church. "Immediately I was attracted to a beautiful, charming little church. There my Beloved, whom I desire to serve, resides."

Francis was a soldier of the emperor, but ultimately he wished to serve the most exalted Master possible, the King of Kings and the Lord of Lords Himself. As God's soldier first, he served the Holy Sacrifice of the Mass in spite of the mockery and ridicule of his comrades. As a faithful servant of the emperor, he was not ashamed to wear his military uniform while performing this sacred service. His faith and convictions were deeply rooted in his soul and built on solid rock. The fickle winds of human respect did not ruffle his feathers. Francis knew what he wanted and what he stood for, and he pursued this with all the strength of his being.

On one occasion Francis injured his knee while on military duty. The wound became infected and required surgery. "After they cleaned the infected wound, they sewed it back together. During the operation I turned my thoughts to the suffering Savior. Glad to be able to offer Him a little suffering, I did not feel much pain." After the operation he had to remain in bed for a few days. His greatest trial was not being able to go to Mass and receive Communion. When First Friday came around he won over his superior by his persistence and Holy Communion was brought to him.

Once he regained his health Francis put all his effort into preparing for the approaching feast of *Corpus Christi* (the feast of the Body and Blood of Christ). Getting a head start, he went through the countryside asking the people for donations of flowers, especially roses. He used the flowers to decorate the procession route and one of the outdoor altars. He went to bed on the eve of the feast very tired yet happy: "By noon I was already exhausted. This was the first time I got really tired in the service of the Most Blessed Sacrament."

Francis the soldier knew how to serve both God and Emperor at the same time. He offered his heart to God. And it would not be long before he sacrificed his physical health and his young life itself for the Emperor's cause as well.

Chapter 6
His "Friend" Death

Sitting down to his diary at the battle front, Francis conversed with a rather unusual "friend," *brother death*: "You are the great friend of humanity, my dear companion and brother. Among us soldiers you are loved very little. Not understanding why you exist, few want to meet you face to face. It seems a well-kept secret that you are the one who will lead us into blessed eternity. In reality only those dread you in whom the love of God and His commandments has grown cold, who have banished sanctifying grace from their hearts by their vices, crimes, and sins, thereby inviting Satan into their souls. Those who grow strong in grace and the love of God, closely following the Savior during their short sojourn on earth, love you and call you their brother and dear friend. And when you arrive to greet them, you lead them to the fulfillment of their heart's desire: Jesus, and the company of the heavenly host.

"My dear and longed-for friend, it is when we renounce all the goods of this world, even our very bodies, that you are able to bear us with ease and swiftness to the ineffable reward of everlasting life. No longer weighed down by the things of this life, we can completely forget them and rejoice in the superabundance and glory of the beatific vision. Thank you for this service of yours, this gift, in return for such a small sacrifice on our part.

"Although I am only a miserable sinner, I would very much like to call you my friend and brother. Even though I have offended God, I have also loved Him as fervently as my weak heart is able. Having offered Him all my abilities and my very life, and entrusting myself entirely to Him, I place my hope in His gracious mercy and forgiveness.

"My dear brother! When you are sent to escort me to my true Homeland, don't bother sending your heralds to alert me to your imminent arrival. Just hold out your hand and lift me up without delay. I will be ready to follow you with joy to my beloved Bridegroom *whenever* you come – *even today or right now*. Thank you for granting my request and for your kind service. *Salve frater* ('Greetings, Brother')!"

Only a cheerful, determined, and pure heart could express such sentiments. Indeed, the virtue which Francis' cheerful soul loved most was purity of heart. Five years had passed since he solemnly promised to be pure, and his ongoing prayer before the tabernacle gave him the strength necessary to resist temptation and to reject vigorously all the vulgarity spewed forth in his presence by his comrades. Purity of heart radiated from his whole being and made a deep impression on everyone. Someone who knew him at this time wrote: "Even now it brings me joy to think of that innocent young man. His bright, brilliant eyes and his childlike countenance shone with a yearning for the things of God." The pure of heart do not fear death; for them death means life. *Blessed are the pure of heart, for they will see God* (Mt. 5:8).

Chapter 7
Holy Week Begins

A sea of light, created by dozens of candles, covered the altar in Saint Blase's Church in Salzburg, Austria, on New Year's day, 1916. Christ was enthroned on the altar for the devotion known as the "forty hours." Among the faithful adorers a soldier kept watch before the Holy of Holies. He asked a favor from the King of Kings and his request was heard. Francis Alexander Kern asked to be showered with suffering.

* * *

On Sunday, September 10, 1916, at 4:30 a.m., a shower of bullets rained down upon the earth. The Italians attacked and weakened the forces of the empire, though they did not prevail. Francis and his platoon took refuge in a cave. They had to leave its protection to bring ammunition to the outpost at 10:00 p.m. One of the soldiers of the platoon was mortally wounded and Francis related, "I found him, alas, when he was already at the point of death and I only had enough time to say the prayers for the dying. I was very sorry I did not arrive sooner. What a sad thing. The artillery is very heavy, and I will have to go to the outpost tonight. God be with me!"

The next day, following his night mission to the outpost, he made a brief entry in his diary: "I was hit by a bullet: my lung and liver were wounded." It was a simple entry, but a life-changing event.

Francis dragged himself back to his platoon and checked in seriously wounded and exhausted. It took two days to get him to a hospital and by then the wound was infected and oozing bloody pus. He had a high fever. In the midst of his agony he *sang*: "Trust my soul, confidently trust in the Lord. He helps those who trust in Him. In trial and distress our faithful God will protect you." The doctors, nurses, and other patients in the room could not restrain their tears when they heard this man at the point of death singing his unwavering trust in God. This day a new chapter in the life of the seminarian-soldier began: his personal Holy Week.

For nine months Francis vacillated between life and death. To reduce the infectious flow, he underwent a first surgery to remove a large piece of one of his ribs. The head-nurse, Princess Schönburg, related how moved she was by Francis' example of patience and faith. Francis was promoted to second lieutenant and given the silver medal for his bravery.

God chastises the son whom He loves (cf. Prv. 3:12, Heb. 12:6, & Rev. 3:19). Francis loved God with his whole heart, soul, mind, and strength. In turn, God loved Francis dearly and sent him painful suffering to purify him like gold refined in the furnace. In the midst of his pain, Francis felt that he was being set free from the bonds which tied him to earth. In this newfound freedom he began to mount swiftly to the summit of perfection.

On one occasion the military chaplain came to Francis' bedside and remarked, "Lieutenant, it looks as if the time of your death is drawing near. Be ready." Mustering all his strength, Francis cried out as loud as he could: "*No!* I don't want to die! I *won't* die, I will become a *priest!*" This young soldier had an incredible determination to ascend the steps of the altar and offer the Eucharistic sacrifice. Only then would he be content to sing with the venerable old Simeon: *Now, Master, you may let your serv-ant go in peace* (Lk. 2:29).

Chapter 8
A Seminarian Again

By October of 1917, Francis was discharged from the military for reasons of health. Despite his weakened condition he could not rest while his heart still longed for the priesthood. He returned to the seminary in Vienna, where he penned the poetic sentiment:

> *O Seminary, my alma mater, dear:*
> *Where peace and joy remain ever near*
> *And hearts are enflamed by God's presence, clear.*

Perceiving that all the hardships and sufferings he had endured up to this point in his life were meant as a preparation for the priesthood, he wrote: "I have suffered. But I couldn't be happier, just like one feels after having done a good deed. Now I can enter the holy realms of the priesthood at least somewhat purified. It has been good for me to get a small taste of the common things in ordinary life, for I have truly seen how little joy is found in them. On the other hand, in spite of scorn and contempt, I have learned how beautiful it is to be enrolled in the school of the Divine Heart."

Right from the start his fellow seminarians were fond of Francis. His spirits remained high in spite of all that he had suffered as a wounded soldier. Unlike the souls where God is not present with His sanctifying grace, Francis' peaceful soul was filled with an abundance of light, generosity, and joy. The war had caused many to fall upon difficult times. Food was strictly rationed. Francis, who had very little himself, still found ways and means to alleviate the need of others. He regularly gave away his ration of bread, and he even used his disability pension to help his needy fellow seminarians.

The war continued to rage on all sides and the number of those encountering *brother death* mounted. As the empire gasped its final breath, every capable man was called by the commanding voice of the emperor to the battlefield. The serene walls of the seminary could not protect the students from this mandatory summons. Once again Lieutenant Kern was obliged to postpone his priestly studies

and enter the cause. Francis wore his roman collar under his military uniform to remind himself constantly who he was and where he was headed. Nothing could suppress his vehement desire to become a priest.

Chapter 9
The Changing of the Guard

The war finally ended in 1918 and the Austro-Hungarian Empire collapsed, leaving in its wake many nations lying around like fallen trees after a violent storm. These nations which had belonged to the empire for centuries, now grew discontent and thirsted for freedom and independence from one another. Considering the instability generated by the war, it did not take much to set the process in motion.

The same revolutionary forces which separated nations after the fall of the empire also attacked the Rock of Peter on which Christ had built His Church with the promise: *The gates of the netherworld shall not prevail against it* (Mt. 16:18). This was particularly true in the newly established "Czechoslovakia," where excessive greed, passion, and nationalism led even priests and religious to abandon the Church of Jesus Christ and to cooperate in the founding of an independent Czech "national church." These disciples of Christ disregarded the inevitable fate of those who separate themselves from His Church and turned their attention to the building of a merely human, national organization.

One of the first leaders of the new "church" was a Norbertine canon named Isidore Bogdan Zahradnik, from the monastery of Strahov in Prague (the abbey where the body of St. Norbert has rested since 1627). Isidore had pledged his loyalty to the Savior as a member of the Norbertine Order and vowed to give himself entirely as a priest and religious. He now disregarded the words of St. Norbert, his Order's father and founder, who said, "Remain here, you who have promised stability in this sacred place, bearing without aversion the continual yoke of God's service" (from the *Sermo Sancti Norberti*). Isidore abandoned his religious community and the Roman Catholic Church, taking many others along with him. The media immediately pounced on the story and published the news far and wide. The enemies of the Church rejoiced in this victory and used it as grist for their propaganda mills: a fallen-away priest and religious was worth his weight in gold to them.

When the news of Isidore's defection reached Francis' ears in Vienna, he was very much affected. His impassioned love for Jesus caused him to grieve for the great offense his Lord suffered and also called forth compassion for the unfortunate schismatic priest. Francis' peace was disturbed by a new storm brewing in his soul, a storm which consistently grew stronger and more powerful. The incident troubled him all the more since, as a soldier, he was now habituated to strict discipline, duty, service, and loyalty. These concepts were no longer mere words to Francis, but sacred obligations. This priest had betrayed his sacred vows!

As the interior storm increased in his soul, so did the interior voice of his heart, until it called out to him commanding loudly and clearly: "Throw yourself into the breach! Take the place of the deserter!" Francis made his decision on the spot: he would make atonement by taking the place of the one who had abandoned his post. He would step into his place as a loyal soldier of Christ and atone for all the harm he had caused.

Francis understood right from the start what such an offering meant. His decision soon took concrete shape when he offered himself to the Norbertine Order which Isidore had deserted. When Francis learned that the Order was especially devoted to the Mother of God, he was all the more anxious to enter. He prepared himself for life-long suffering, certain that Christ would accept his offering. And later on, when his sufferings were practically unbearable, he never regretted the total gift of himself as a sacrificial soul.

Francis brought his desire to his spiritual director without delay. This prudent priest, Father Karl Handlos, decided to test Francis' resolve and did not let him enter right away. He did not want Francis to regret this as a rash action later in life and he wanted to see if a little time would strengthen and solidify this unique call. A year later, convinced that it was God's will, Father Handlos gave Francis his blessing to enter the Norbertine Order as a sacrificial soul. After a year of holding back and repeating in his heart, "*Non in commotione, Domine*" ("*Not in the whirlwind, Lord,*" *but in calm*) (cf. 1 Kings 19:11), Francis was now permitted to step into the vacated position of Isidore and offer atonement to God through complete loyalty and immolation.

Chapter 10
Our Lady of Geras

The Norbertines are also known as the "Premonstratensians," after the location of their mother abbey in the valley of Prémontré, France. This priestly Order is dedicated to the solemn celebration of the Liturgy and the chanting of the Divine Office and is known for its devotion to the Blessed Sacrament and the Virgin Mother of God. The Order also focuses on life in common for its priests, pastoral ministry, and the education of youth.

The Norbertine abbey of Geras is nestled in a forest far from the hectic pace of the world (about a four-hour walk from Horn and not far from the border of the Czech Republic). The abbey was founded by count Ulrich of Pernegg in 1153 with Norbertines who came from the abbey of Želiv in Bohemia (a daughter house of the abbey of Steinfeld in Germany). The abbey's church was elevated to the rank of a Minor Basilica in 1953.

In 1947 Isfrid Franz, a former abbot of Geras, wrote in his book, *The History of the Monastery in the Forest District: Geras-Pernegg*: "Poverty is plentiful in the history of our abbey. Nevertheless, in our eight-hundred years of existence God has blessed us in His good pleasure by continually sending young men to pledge their lives to Him at the *House of Holy Mary of Geras*. Through their faithful lives and hard work, God has always extended His helping hand to us. This abbey has hidden a few saints within its walls: the happy result of the religious life." Although the abbey, which was once totally destroyed, was no stranger to suffering, it never ceased to experience the powerful protection of Mary, who lovingly cared for her house at Geras. There is even a miraculous statue above the main altar of the church known as *"Our Blessed Lady of Geras."*

The history of this statue goes back to 1517 when Martin Luther began to preach a "new gospel," which swept across Germany like a storm wind. A frenzy of *"evangelical freedom"* took hold of the people and led them to interpret the articles of faith as they wished. The German nobility played an important leadership role in this movement and succeeded in poisoning the peasants with pamphlets ridiculing and mocking the Catholic faith and its priests.

Abbot Paul Linsbauer was the spiritual head of Geras at this time. He was both a powerful leader and a spiritual father entirely loyal to the Church. In the year 1520, with devotion to the Blessed Mother threatened by the errors spreading on every side, he erected the statue of her above the main altar that remains a jewel of the abbey church to this day.

Confusion and disaster continued to spread and it seemed that there would never again be peace. The Thirty Years War raged. Exactly a century after the erection of the statue, in January of 1620, a group of thirty men on horseback from nearby Raabs plundered the abbey. They drove all 545 sheep away, took everything of value, and set the abbey and its church on fire. The fire spread to the nearby village and raged for days, leaving everything in ruins. Those priests who were able escaped with a few possessions to Drosendorf. Everyone else was taken captive and never heard from again. Geras was dealt what appeared to be a fatal blow. With the village plundered and torched, and the monastery and its land destroyed, all hope seemed lost.

The five years of desolation that followed saw a few glimmers of hope when the Catholic Reformation began to make a difference. Emperor Ferdinand was able to take back the Protestant strongholds one by one. Also at this time five of the priests who escaped Geras returned to the ruins. They begged for their bread, with the sky as the roof over their heads. When they began the work of clearing the rubble from church, they were amazed to discover that the carved wooden statue of the Blessed Mother was still completely intact above the ruins of the former altar. She had been placed there by the abbot 105 years earlier. The abbey and its church rose again from the ashes with her protection and help.

The annals of the abbey relate that during the time of Abbot Peter Herkard (1632-1650) pilgrimages were revived to honor the Blessed Virgin at the request of the emperor. During the reign of the next abbot, John Westhaus (1650-1674), the annals state: "The Catholic Reformation saw a triumphant marching forth of priests, including the Norbertines, who conducted missions throughout the land. The abbey of Geras became a center of spiritual renewal, especially in regard to devotion to the Blessed Mother. The abbot loved the Blessed Virgin with a special love, and her feasts were celebrated with extra solemnity. The venerable statue of Mary was now honored as miraculous because of all that it had survived. Great numbers of the faithful came to honor her, especially on her principal local feast of the Visitation (celebrated on July 2 at that time)." It was in such an abbey, in such a church, in accord with God's beautiful plan of providence, that Francis Alexander Kern, the priest of atonement, would find his niche.

Chapter 11
A New Man, a New Life

Although Francis had never been to Geras and had no previous connection with the abbey, he knew it was God's will for him to enter Geras the moment he heard of its existence from a friend. He left his beloved Vienna behind and became a novice, receiving the white habit of the Order from Abbot Emilian Greisl. The reception of the religious habit is the putting on of a "new man." No external remnant of the "old man" of the world is to remain, not even his name. Francis received the new religious name "James," after the Norbertine martyr St. James Lacoupe, who was hung to death by Calvinist pirates in 1572.

James focused primarily on his spiritual life during the novitiate year. He wrote to his sister that the novitiate was a great comfort to him, because he had never before found the time to enter into a sustained dialogue with Jesus. Throughout the intensive year of spiritual training, James was exposed to the fundamental themes of religious life, including death to self and separation from the world. The novitiate also introduced the young novice to the history of the Order and the spirit of its holy fathers, Saints Augustine and Norbert. James implored the Blessed Virgin of Geras to help him grow in the life of perfection during this year and took special joy in decorating the altars of the abbey church where her miraculous image was enshrined.

James' abbot later wrote of him: "Having a strong devotion to the Sacred Heart, the concept of atonement was deeply rooted in James' soul. He strengthened this idea by joining the Society of Sacrificial Souls. These souls gave themselves without reserve to the will of the Sacred Heart of Jesus. They promised to accept all physical and spiritual sufferings sent by the Divine Heart in a spirit of humble repentance."

James professed his first vows on October 20, 1921, promising poverty, chastity and obedience for three years. On the occasion the abbot noted in his sermon that profession confirms the calling to community life which has been tested in the novitiate. He compared James to a newly lit candle on account of his exemplary practice of virtue. James, for his part, professed his vows with utter sincerity and joyfully offered his entire self to God – intellect, will, heart, and body – in the abbey of Geras. As he knelt before the altar, he was happier than he had ever been. And he went on to live these vows fully and faithfully until his dying breath.

Abbot Emilian sent James back to his hometown after his profession to complete his theological studies at the University of Vienna. The "little boy" from Vienna had completed the first stage of his ascent to the holy mountain.

Chapter 12
"I Will Go Unto the Altar of God"

Only one thing remained for James now, the summit of happiness and the fulfillment of all his desires: the holy priesthood. After completing the necessary studies, James was ordained to the priesthood on July 23, 1922, at Saint Stephen's Cathedral in Vienna. He knelt prayerfully before Cardinal Archbishop Friedrich Gustav Piffl, who laid hands on his head while the Savior Himself impressed an indelible mark on His newest priest's soul. James' longing was satisfied at last as he realized the culmination of so many sacrifices and prayers. His heart sang joyfully to the Lord, Who lovingly looked upon His newest priest. James was now, in the literal sense, *father*, and *alter Christus* (*another Christ*).

August 1, 1922, was the day scheduled for James' first offering of the Holy Sacrifice of the Mass. For the newly ordained priest it was the fulfillment of an intense and sustained yearning, and the crown of momentous struggles and suffering. Abbot Emilian permitted James to celebrate the solemn Mass at the sister's convent in Vöcklabruck, where he first visited in 1915. James had been received there with generous hospitality long before he knew of the abbey at Geras. The sisters rejoiced in his visits and always treated him as a son.

James himself, out of gratitude to the Sisters and people of the village, had earlier procured a precious reliquary for the church's altar and installed a new lighting system which highlighted the reliquary and the altar. The Sisters and villagers now responded by adorning the church splendidly for his first Mass. Excitement ran high as everyone prepared to welcome the young priest. Even though he had no roots or relations here, the village had been an oasis for him during his military service and the people had come to know and love him. They arrived for the celebration decked out in their full folk costumes, with a spontaneous outpouring of love and honor.

Abbot Emilian arranged to have James driven the day before the Mass in a wagon bedecked with white flowers. His room resembled

a rose garden. The night before the celebration he was haunted by a familiar concern, wondering whether he would live till the day of his first Mass. He had often prayed, "Dear God, let me live to offer the Holy Sacrifice of the Mass at least once." At the last minute, just before Mass, he vomited blood. But he overcame his frail body with a fierce will and holy enthusiasm and celebrated the Mass without incident. Everyone present was profoundly struck by the noble beauty and holy grandeur of this pure, devout priest celebrating his first Mass. One non-Catholic in attendance said, "Only love can accomplish such things." James himself later wrote of this day, "My first Mass was filled with jubilation. It was like Palm Sunday and Jesus' entry into Jerusalem. Now I am entering my Holy Week."

Chapter 13
In the Lord's Vineyard

In addition to making reparation, there was a further motive for James' choice of the Norbertine Order. His humility drew him to a quiet, inconspicuous position where he would be little noticed. This corresponded well with the life of the Norbertines at Geras who devoted themselves to the care of the simple, modest people in the local villages. Father James now willingly accepted any and every hardship in order to minister to these people and lead them to God.

As a deacon, James had already preached his first public sermon in the Basilica of Our Lady of Geras on July 11, 1922 (at that time the principal feast of Saint Norbert). A few days after his first Mass he preached in the small pilgrimage church of Mary of the Snows by Drosendorf. He also preached frequently in the abbey's basilica where the number of those who came to hear him grew steadily.

Fr. James was often called upon to preach in the churches of the outlying villages. He readily accepted, even though he knew he could have a violent hemorrhage at any moment. He took his pastoral obligations seriously and traveled to these various churches in good weather and bad, in fall and winter, despite the fact that he frequently spat blood. He was often forced to sit down exhausted during the Mass. But the deep faith and fiery devotion with which he celebrated the Sacred Mysteries were clearly evident and moving.

James was an excellent preacher. Everything he said came from the heart, springing forth from his deep faith. He had a great gift for awakening the sleeping faith of his listeners, as evidenced by the fact that so many souls who heard him were touched to seek reconciliation with God and the Church and the number of those in line for his confessional increased.

James would not let bad weather or other hardships interfere with his visits to the local schools to teach religion. He zealously lived out the words of Jesus, *Let the children come to me* (Mt. 19:14). His whole heart went out to them, seeking to plant the seed of God's word in their hearts and nurturing them as they grew. Father James did not limit himself to the scheduled class times, but spent much of his own free time with the children and even organized a Marian group to lead the children to Jesus through Mary. He also gave generously of his time to help form young men into fervent Catholics and good citizens, organizing them into a Catholic association for this purpose.

James exemplified genuine Christian love of neighbor through his compassionate care for the sick. He was often found consoling the suffering and praying with the infirm. If he was called to administer the last rites, no distance was too far and no hour too late. In spite of his own weak health, he hurried along, praying with a strong voice along the way in the company of those who joined him.

James' most beloved task, however, was bringing lost sheep back to the Father's fold through the ministry of the confessional. He devoted himself to each person with great love and earnestly sought to reconcile each one with God. He refreshed many tired, weary souls and reconciled many sinners. James would often pass by a particular image of "the silent priest of Prague," Saint John Nepomuk, while out walking. This saint had died as a martyr for protecting the seal of confession. Every time James saw the statue on a bridge near the abbey he prayed, "Lord, You may take everything else from me, but give me souls." Only in heaven will it be known just how many people received the balm of God's mercy from his hands and returned to the love of God through his priestly ministry of reconciliation.

Chapter 14
The Priest of Atonement

The course of Blessed James' life on earth was running swiftly to its conclusion. The closer he drew to his end, the more his sufferings intensified. In a penitential spirit, he offered everything to God.

James caught a cold in the confessional at Eastertime which made him cough and spit blood severely. He still preached on the first of May, but he hemorrhaged violently the day after and this episode was soon followed by another. At the same time his chest wound became infected again, discharging pus and becoming so bad that he was taken to the hospital on August 10, 1923. Some of his ribs had to be removed. Due to the weak condition of his heart, the surgery was done without anesthesia. James endured the horrific pain for two hours, during which he bit through a towel without making a sound. Although the pain was incredible, when the surgeon told James that he would have to take out a fourth rib after he had removed the first three, James jokingly apologized for being so much trouble.

As soon as he was able to get up again, James visited the other patients in the hospital to bless them. He consoled them with compassionate humor and made them smile. The heroism with which he endured his suffering was astonishing. A Sacred Heart Sister from Vienna who took care of him at this time said she was deeply moved and edified by James' piety, patience, virile spirit, humility, and sincere gratitude.

Following the surgery and his moderate recovery he went to Southern Tyrol to spend the winter recuperating. James hoped to return to his pastoral duties at the abbey in the spring and worked hard to regain his health during the winter at the Marian hospice in Meran. He won the hearts of the sisters and other patients during this time of convalescence through his constant cheerfulness and childlike piety. Even as a patient in the hospital he could not remain idle and always sought to minister to immortal souls.

In his first letter from Meran he mentioned that the chapel was only a few steps from his room. A few weeks later he wrote, "I am very happy each day that I am able to pray part of the Divine Office again. To pray the whole Office at this time would be too difficult and I have to avoid all exertion. But being allowed to serve at the altar every day and to have the Savior for a neighbor is the crowning of all that is good and beautiful. It is a glorious compensation for the little suffering that I bear."

Christmas shed a ray of hope and he was delighted with the modest celebration prepared by the sisters. He did not pass up the opportunity to say a few words, turning everyone's hearts to the Infant Jesus. He later wrote in his diary, "After dinner the two large folding doors of the hall opened and a magnificent Christmas tree shone brightly. Little girls dressed as angels performed a fitting Christmas play in front of the crib. After we sang Christmas songs I said a few words about the peace and joy of Christmas. On Christmas Day I celebrated the three Holy Masses without any ill effects on my health. I gave a ten-minute sermon at Mass on New Year's Day."

James continued to recuperate slowly over the next months. Even though it must have been a great strain for him, he sang a High Mass and preached on Easter Sunday. He wrote, "I was very happy. Even if I, a young priest, have to sit with my hands in my lap to rest as needed, it is still a great consolation after all the bitter hours of being sick."

James headed home to Geras in late spring with his health and strength satisfactorily restored. He stopped on the way in Salzburg to visit his aunt. She later wrote of his stay, "When Father James visited on his way from Meran for a day and an evening, I had to change the dressing on his wound twice. He said that if I didn't get nauseated and it wouldn't bother me too much he would appreciate me changing the dressing. I was shocked when I saw how the pus flowed from his wound like sewage from a sewer-pipe, and I said, 'You poor, poor martyr!' He replied with great earnestness, 'I'm not poor. Don't you know that in every age God always needs some people to do the work and others to suffer? If the Savior appointed me to suffer, then I am ready to do it as long as it is His will.'"

These sentiments were reminiscent of Jesus in the garden of Gethsemane when He prayed in His agony, *Father, if you are willing, take this cup away from me; still, not my will but yours be done* (Lk. 22:42). James Kern was willing to continue suffering as long as Jesus, the Eternal High Priest of Atonement, desired. The suffering Lord on the cross was his model and strength. "Lord, Thy will be done, and let the pain be just as much as you will. Lord, Thy will be done – even if it seems to hurt too much at times."

Chapter 15
"In Everything Give Thanks"

Saint Joseph is beautifully praised in the simple words of Saint Matthew's Gospel as *vir justus*, *"a just man"* (cf. Mt. 1:19). The same could be said of James Kern, who practiced the virtue of justice to a heroic degree. He always strove to be faithful to God, observing the commandments, the precepts of the Church, and the duties of his state in even the smallest details. He never took the credit for himself, recognizing the work of God's grace in all aspects of his life. He honored the Blessed Virgin Mary with childlike devotion and chose St. Joseph and St. Jude as special intercessors. He also had a great reverence for the angels and saints.

James was always faithful to the Church by conscientiously observing her commandments, teachings, and discipline. He consistently respected the rights and dignity of his fellow man. Whenever he gave his word he was anxious to keep it. On one occasion he told his sister, "Mimi, you know that I had to take an oath to do my duty and put my life on the line as a soldier for the fatherland. This applies now even more since I received the unspeakable blessing of the priesthood. I made a solemn promise and am ready at any moment to give my life for God."

Above all else James was immensely grateful to God for His many kindnesses and did whatever he could to lead others toward the recognition of the need for giving thanks to God. During his stay at Meran he met a convert from Denmark who gave him a litany of thanksgiving composed by another convert, a Danish priest. The prayer was entitled *A Litany of Abundant Thanksgiving to God* (cf. Appendix III, pg. 70). It was a magnificent prayer of gratitude to God for His wondrous gifts of nature and grace. James was deeply touched by the litany. He had often wondered how best to cultivate sentiments of thanksgiving in souls. His innermost desire was that all living things give praise to God. Hence, he had ten thousand copies of the litany published. But God would call him from this world before he was able to distribute it.

Chapter 16

His Last Sermon

Upon his return to Geras, James took up the care of souls once again as much as his health permitted. He was able to do so for only a short time before his health deteriorated again. He continued to preach as long as he still had a little strength left. He preached his last sermon on July 20, 1924, at the celebration of the priestly jubilee of the bishop of the diocese of St. Pölten. James preached on the virtue of loyalty to the Church and her supreme shepherd. He had a firm and profound love for the Church and an understanding of her as the sole guide to the Savior and eternal salvation. It is noteworthy that this was his last sermon before he was silenced by his incredibly painful sufferings.

As the sermon drew to an end he declared, "Either we remain loyal to our bishop, and thus to Christ, or we flirt with dissent and the fires of hell. My dear friends, if you are willing to accept Jesus' teaching of the unadulterated truth and live by it, then remain with us. If you are willing to acknowledge Jesus Christ as your shepherd and high priest, first seek His priestly blessing of reconciliation before you bring your gift to the altar. Then you belong here; you may remain with us. It is here that the Eternal High Priest prepares His banquet and invites you to His table.

"My dear friends, if you desire to practice moral heroism as soldiers of the Holy Spirit, the arsenal stockpiled with courage and perseverance for the spiritual combat is to be found only here. In union with the Church here on earth you will find the successor of the chief of the apostles. And when you die, you will find the eternal Shepherd of your souls in heaven Who will give you, His chosen ones, the crown of life.

"If however your ear delights in falsehood, in the poisonous whisperings of the modern paganism which says, 'There is no God, no hereafter, and no sin;' if this is the tune you prefer, *then get up quickly and leave this place* (cf. Jn. 13:27), for you do not belong here. What are you looking for here? You were made to be temples and soldiers of the Holy Spirit, yet you desecrate yourselves, your immortal souls, by obstinately living a sinful life. Get off the narrow road which leads to life. Go out and take the wide, comfortable, and easy road where you can follow your every whim. But know without doubt that you will be accompanied by those whom you dread and yet deserve – the devil and all his minions."

This was James' final ascent to the pulpit in his beloved abbey church. He would soon ascend to a much higher pulpit above the clouds! His health failed. Once again there was a large amount of pus in his chest wound. He was taken to the hospital in Vienna for another surgery in September during which four more ribs were removed. This did not take care of the problem, and another surgery was scheduled as soon as he regained a little strength. The servant of God predicted that he would not awaken after this final surgery.

Chapter 17
Home to God

As his last moments on earth drew near, the twenty-seven-year-old priest and religious prepared for his homecoming. This time of preparation, leading up to the next surgery on October 20, 1924, was both the climax of his sufferings and the greatest unfolding and flowering of his noble soul and its generous willingness to sacrifice.

In addition to severe bodily pain, spiritual suffering became James' companion. One day during this period he admitted, "Now all consolation is gone." He added immediately, "Since it is God's will, I am not sad about it." Eight days before his death a good friend came to visit him and noticed that his ever-cheerful expression suddenly changed. A shadow slipped over his face. "I took his hand," the friend later wrote, "and asked him what he was thinking." James replied, "It is so difficult. It was easier to endure before, but now it is almost impossible. All the reasons I had been giving others and myself have begun to lose their force of persuasion." A short pause ensued during which the friend was trying to think of something consoling or encouraging to say. Then James continued with tears filling his eyes, "This is happening only because God's love permits it and because I love Him so much."

During the first surgery it was discovered that his pleura (the membranous sacs enveloping the lungs which reduce the friction of the lungs during respiration) were entirely black and infected. In spite of the unbearable pain this caused him (especially when he breathed), James remained calm, quiet, and self-controlled. He never expressed any personal needs or took any painkillers. He wanted to bring his sacrifice free and unsullied to its consummation. He took whatever nourishment was given him without being fussy or particular, never indicating what he wanted to eat, though he must have had special needs due to his high fever and intense pain. No one knew if what they had given him agreed with him. James' consistent cheerfulness amazed and edified the sisters who cared for him and everyone else who happened to see him during this time.

In a great irony of providence, Monday, October 20, 1924, the day scheduled by his doctors for his surgery, was also the day he was slated to make his final profession of vows in the Norbertine Order. Unable to change the day of the surgery, he had to postpone making his solemn vows and content himself with renewing his temporary vows shortly before the operation. Days earlier he had told one of the sisters, "I will be celebrating the day of my profession in heaven." Two days prior to the operation he told his aunt, "I will not awaken from the surgery on Monday." And on Sunday evening he said, "Tomorrow at this time I will see the Blessed Mother and my Guardian Angel."

That evening, while a sister was preparing the small altar on which he would receive Holy Communion before the surgery, he asked her, "Would you please be kind enough to prepare everything beautifully, because the last communion should be celebrated as solemnly as the first. Tomorrow I will receive my last communion and celebrate my solemn profession in heaven." Then he asked her to bring his white religious habit and see to it that everything was fittingly arranged. He explained how the habit was to be put on so he would be properly dressed in his coffin. The sister was deeply moved by the calm and matter-of-fact manner with which he said this.

A holy joy shone on his face as he serenely resigned himself to God's will in the hours before his death. Before being wheeled into surgery he blessed his relatives, benefactors and friends. As he was wheeled away he called out happily, "I will not return!" In fact, he did not. During the surgery, after the hospital chaplain had given him the Last Rites and the Apostolic Blessing, James died as he foretold.

The priest of atonement's life on earth was over. But his work for souls was to continue. From heaven he accomplishes what he could not during his short life on earth. He continues to lead souls, many souls to Jesus!

Chapter 18
In the Cemetery of Geras

The body of the servant of God, dressed in his white Norbertine habit, was brought to the morgue of Vienna's General Hospital where the first funeral rite was celebrated on Wednesday, October 22nd, at 1:30 p.m., in the presence of many priests and lay people. His body was then taken back to the community he so dearly loved, his home at Geras, where he had become a religious and initiated his holy mission as a priest of atonement in the Norbertine Order.

The widely read Christian daily newspaper *Reichspost* noted that there was a large turnout for the burial of this beloved and respected young priest. The solemn *Requiem* Mass was celebrated by Abbot Emilian Greisl at 10 a.m. on October 25th. Many of his Catholic Fraternity brothers were present. Some of them were pall bearers while others carried their Fraternity banner. In addition to all the priests who traveled to attend his funeral, a representative of the Cardinal-Archbishop of Vienna was also present. Gathered together in more of a triumphal march than a funeral procession, the people of Geras and the surrounding villages accompanied the body on its last pilgrimage to the abbey's section of the beautiful forest cemetery. James was buried above a confrere who had died sixty years earlier and a brick vault was placed over the casket. On the plaque in the cemetery wall the image of a chalice with a host was engraved with the words: *Hic Requiescunt: R. D. Adalbertus Pelikan, O. Praem., 1784-1864. R. D. Jacobus Franciscus Kern, O. Praem., 1897, def. 20. Octobris 1924, miles laesus* (Here rest: Father Adalbert Pelikan, Norbertine, 1784-1864, and Father James Francis Kern, Norbertine, [born] 1897, died the 20th of October 1924, having been wounded as a soldier).

Chapter 19
A Reputation for Holiness

James Kern was already spoken of as a saint during his lifetime. This was the case all the more after his death and his reputation for holiness has grown ever since. As a child he was called "one of God's favored children," "an angel," and "a little saint." At the archdiocesan minor seminary in Hollabrunn his fellow students respected his practice of the virtues. Those with whom he fought in the First World War called him their "guardian angel" and their "intercessor with God." Among his fellow seminarians in Vienna there were also some who considered him a saint.

Many of his confreres at the abbey of Geras, especially the abbot, regarded him as God's chosen one and a special child of St. Norbert and his Order. James was a "holy person and holy priest" to the sisters in Vöcklabruck. The people of Geras and the nearby region referred to him as "the saintly Father James." Probably those who witnessed his heroic sufferings firsthand were the most convinced that they had a saint among them. To obtain his relics, a number of priests and sisters took parts of the ribs which had been removed in the surgery and enshrined them as belonging to a "priest who died with a reputation for holiness."

One of James' priest-friends wrote a short summary of his life and published it in the *Wiener Kirchenblatt*. He wrote, "The life of the deceased can be a model for everyone: for some, he is a model in which to find consolation and strength; for others, a stimulus and inspiration for more intense and fervent love; and for others, perhaps, an urgent call to interior contemplation." He continued, "Those who had a close glimpse into his life and intimate contact with him know with certitude that he lived a holy life." In conclusion he stated, "This holy priest is an example of virtue that shines for us and, during our difficult and trying hours, inspires us with courage, strength, consolation, and love."

In summary, James epitomized that priestly holiness so dear to the heart of St. Norbert. Everyone who knew him was certain that he was a saint, and this sure knowledge continued to spread throughout the countryside and the world.

Chapter 20
Thirty Years Later

As the years slipped by, the abbots of Geras were approached repeatedly to initiate the beatification process, but other more immediate needs kept interfering. It became necessary to place everything in God's hands, entrusting the cause of James Kern directly to Him when more practical earthly matters took precedence. The first of these was economic in nature. Shortly after James' death the abbey ran into serious financial trouble. Emilian Greisl, the abbot who had received James into the order and a man of silent modesty and deep spirituality, struggled to handle this difficulty properly, but his well-meaning attempts fell short and he resigned two years later in 1926.

Ludolph Rudisch, elected abbot in 1927, only lived three years and never had the time to initiate the beatification process. Friedrich Silberhauer was elected abbot in 1931 and reigned for a long time (until 1952), but he endured the destruction of the Second World War, during which the abbey itself was confiscated by the Nazis in 1940 and the community driven away. For five years the buildings were used as a resettlement camp, and were extensively damaged by the end of the war.

In 1947 Isfrid Franz, then pastor of Eibenstein on the Thaya and later elected abbot of Geras, wrote in his book *The History of the Monastery in the Forest District: Geras-Pernegg*, "The flames of distress are blazing high out of the old monastery, just as long ago the flames burst through and consumed the old abbey church. Yet the statue of the Madonna remains steadfast and smiling. This time too, Mary will help us overcome the destruction and woe. Once again a grateful community will gather to celebrate on her altar a sacrifice of thanksgiving to the honor and everlasting praise of God."

Thirty years elapsed before James' beatification process was introduced. Only when Cardinal Theodore Innitzer, the archbishop of Vienna, joined with other petitioners did Abbot Isfrid Franz promise to take the necessary steps. The year was 1955 and the announcement of his intention met with great joy and delight.

Chapter 21
The First Step Toward Canonization

On Wednesday, September 26, 1956, the first step toward canonization was taken: James' body was exhumed. The chronicler relates that after receiving the necessary permission, the abbot, several priests, and two doctors opened the vault and beheld his wooden coffin with the brass plaque inscribed, "Reverend James Kern, died 20 Oct. 1924 in his 28th year." When the wooden coffin was touched it fell apart to reveal the pewter coffin beneath. Through the window of the pewter coffin they were able to see its contents clearly. One of the priests who had known James well exclaimed, "This is he! Yes, it is he!"

On opening the pewter coffin it became impossible to lift the skeleton out in one piece, first of all because the bones fell apart when the coffin was opened and also because the lower portion of the coffin was completely corroded. There were remnants of some skin and hair on the skull and some flesh on the bones. His funeral cross and some of his clothes were still intact. His right hand (the one he used to bless), was still connected to his lower arm and totally preserved to the wrist including the tendons and nails. The effect of his chest surgeries was evidenced by the missing ribs.

The doctors found all the bones of the skeleton intact with the exception of a single ankle bone. They wrapped them in a white linen cloth and placed them in an oak coffin. The coffin was secured with screws and sealed tightly with a crosswise band and the seal of the abbey. The original brass plaque was transferred to the top of the crosswise band. After the abbot closed the windows of the cemetery chapel, he blessed James' remains, locked the door from the outside, and affixed his seal on the door.

The following Sunday, the 30th of September, the relics were transferred to the abbey church. After verifying the seal on the door of the cemetery chapel, the abbot opened the door. The new oak coffin was placed on a flower-adorned bier and carried by the abbey's seminarians to the front of the cemetery chapel where the abbot blessed it. A long procession made its way to the basilica, composed of choir boys followed by the clergy of various ranks,

then the abbot and his assistants robed in black vestments, and finally the seminarians with the bier. Members of the Catholic Fraternity to which James had belonged and the union of all Catholic fraternities in Austria also accompanied the bier. Although the transfer was little publicized, many came from far and wide including government officials, religious sisters, and a large number of the lay faithful.

When the procession entered the basilica a phenomenon occurred that has no natural explanation. A bright ray of light streamed out of the tabernacle and remained until the bier came to rest inside the church. When the solemn pontifical *Requiem* was completed, the coffin was placed in the basilica's rear wall on the left side next to the door and was blessed. His fraternity placed a band of its colors on the coffin, and over the vault the abbot placed a stone plaque inscribed, "Here lies the servant of God, JAMES KERN, born 1897, died 1924."

Chapter 22
The Priestly Hand of Blessing

There is something extraordinary about the consecrated hands of a priest. The Christian people, respecting and loving those hands, know that they must ask the Lord to provide many consecrated hands *"lest the praises cease at Your altars; lest the light before Your tabernacle burn out; lest the sacrifice upon the consecrated altar stone discontinue; lest Your people lack preachers of Your will, shepherds of Your way, and mediators of Your grace."*

The totally preserved right arm and hand of James Kern did not so much surprise people as increase their devotion for the one whom they already considered a saint. Was it pointing to heaven once again to exhort, inspire, and warn, crying out for conversion and pointing the way?

The notes written by James with that same hand just before his ordination to the subdiaconate read, "What is a soul? It is greater than the whole realm of nature and so magnificent that, if necessary and possible, the Savior would be crucified and put to death for it all over again. The Lord honors and values a soul so highly that, not wanting servitude and forced love, He never violates its free will by force.

"Each of us has to save his own soul first. If we lose this opportunity, we will never have it again. Living only one life, there is only one life in which to save our soul. And all is lost if our soul is lost!

"God's creatures, by their very existence, point to the God who made them. The wonderful laws of nature, arranging everything so beautifully, glorify their Creator who must be all the more beautiful. Placing everything in the service of God and of love of neighbor, we must serve God in His creation.

"It is possible to make good use of created things without getting trapped and lost in them. However, if anything leads to sin or is used sinfully, it must be avoided. Never make use of God's creation to cut yourself off from Him, even when trials come. Some things we must suffer and endure patiently: our neighbor, work, sickness, cloudy days, trouble, and distress. When I die I will not say that creation is bad. Instead I will say what God said at the end of the six days of creation: ...*and everything was very good* (Gn. 1:31).

"At the hour of our death heaven's door will either be opened or bolted shut. In the latter case we have forged the bolt by our sins. Any unrepented venial sin is incompatible with the love of God and prepares us at the very least for a long stay in purgatory. Venial sins act like a poison which little by little, dose after dose, endangers the health of the soul. Sickening and weakening the soul to the point of infirmity, venial sins pave the way to mortal sin."

In our own age it seems that we have forgotten the message of James' beseeching, outstretched hand. His hand continues to gesture, pointing us toward heaven. This priest of atonement still has a mission to accomplish.

Chapter 23
God Needs Men!

James Kern, whose life we have sketched, does not rest even after death. He continues interceding for us and guiding us from heaven by the shining example of his life: a life of sacrifice and renunciation in a world of selfishness and self-indulgence. In order to reach his destination of life with God in heaven, he lived his life on earth following the two-fold path of sacrifice and zeal for souls. He always sought to avoid the confusion and despair of life here below, setting his heart on the dazzling heights alone.

Whenever a soul seeks to draw near to God it is a feast day of the spirit! An hour for celebration! This little book is meant to be a thunderous pealing of bells, a crying out to the souls who read it, an urgent invitation to join in the joy of the feast. It is personally addressed to you, the reader, to the noblest place in your heart and soul. Blessed James Kern, the priest of atonement, like an experienced mountain guide, leads the way to the heights for any who desire to follow. He calls out to you to follow him, to climb higher. Above, up ahead, shine the beautiful white-capped peaks of purity, truth, and love: the life of the Norbertine canons. Below, behind you, lay the valleys of indifference, lukewarmness, and self-love: a region from which it would be difficult to reach even purgatory.

The sacrificial life of this young priest is truly a fitting model for our times of selfishness and aversion to sacrifice. It stimulates the life of grace in both young and old, that they might give themselves more generously in service to God and man. About a year before his death, while recovering in Meran, James wrote to his abbot, "If I am allowed to be even just a little wheel in God's plan for the world, then I shall be exceedingly joyful." What a noble proposition: to be a very small wheel in the plan of providence, drawing closer to God, leading and drawing others always forward and upward, and always becoming more noble and holy oneself! As Blessed James himself put it, "God always needs people, some for work and others for suffering." God also needs *you*. God is also calling *you*. Seek Blessed James' intercession and follow him to the heights.

Epilogue
A Blessed Witness to Priestly Fidelity

On a radiant first summer's day and Sunday morning, June 21, 1998, Pope John Paul II arrived in Vienna's *Heldenplatz* (Heroes' Square) to celebrate the beatification of James Francis Kern and two other Austrians, Anton Maria Schwartz and Restituta Kafka. Referring to the plaza in which tens of thousands had gathered for the joyful celebration, the Holy Father exclaimed, "It is not the heroes of this world who have the last word today here in Heroes' Square, but the heroes of the Church: the three new Blessed. About sixty years ago, from a balcony which opens onto this square, a man [named Adolph Hitler] proclaimed himself to be the salvation of the people. The new Blessed bear a very different message: salvation [*Heil*] is not found in any man. Rather, salvation [*Heil*] is found in Christ, the King and Savior of the human race!"

Pope John Paul continued his words with a summary of the life and deeds of Blessed James:

"James Kern came from a modest Viennese working family. The First World War put a sudden end to his studies at the Minor Seminary in Hollabrunn. A serious wound suffered in the war made his brief earthly existence in the Major Seminary and in the Norbertine monastery of Geras a *Holy Week*, as he himself described it. Out of love for Christ he did not selfishly cling to life, but consciously offered it for the good of others. In the beginning he wanted to become a diocesan priest. But an event took place which caused him to change his mind. When a Norbertine priest abandoned his monastery, following the Czech national church which had just recently organized itself in separation from Rome, James Kern discovered his true vocation in this sad event. He wanted to repair the harm done by that religious. James Kern entered the same Order in the monastery of Geras to take his place, and the Lord accepted the offering of the 'substitute.'

"Blessed James Kern presents himself to us as a witness of fidelity to the priesthood. In the beginning it was the desire of his childhood, manifested in his imitation of the priest at the altar. Over time this desire matured. Through a process of painful purification, the profound meaning of his priestly vocation became apparent: to unite his own life to the sacrifice of Christ on the Cross and to offer it in substitution for the salvation of others.

"May Blessed James Kern, who was both a vivacious and serious student, encourage many young men to respond generously to Christ's call to the priesthood. Blessed James' words then still have relevance for us now: 'Today more than ever we have need of authentic and holy priests. Every prayer, every sacrifice, every effort, and every suffering united to the right intention, becomes a divine seed which sooner or later will bear its fruit.' Thank you, Blessed James Kern, for your priestly fidelity!"

Later that same day, as he led the pilgrims in the prayer of the *Angelus*, the Holy Father added, "The three new Blessed confided themselves and their prayers to the maternal intercession of Mary. In order to fulfill different missions, all three said the 'yes' which Mary gave as her response to the message of the angel. Blessed James Kern said 'yes' in the face of the sickness and suffering which came upon him, notwithstanding his young age. May the three new Blessed be for all of you a model and stimulus for saying 'yes' to whatever way God is calling each of you to serve Him."

At the time of the beatification, the remains of Blessed James were transferred from the tomb where they had rested since 1956 to a new memorial chapel on the abbey grounds. The bones were washed, wrapped, and interred in a silver reliquary chest engraved with his name and years of birth and death. It is here, in this chapel, that today's pilgrim comes to experience uniquely the presence and intercession of the priest of atonement once again.

Appendix I:
List of Illustrations

Appendix II:

PRAYER IN HONOR OF BLESSED JAMES

Loving and merciful Father,
We praise and thank You
for showering the world with light and love
through the life and suffering of Your faithful priest,
Blessed James.
Through his intercession
may our priests grow daily in holiness of life.
Through our works of humble penance and reparation,
may we help to restore the balance
destroyed by sin and infidelity
and come at last into Your marvelous light
to share the company of Blessed James
and all Your holy ones.
We ask this through Christ our Lord.
Amen.

Appendix III:

Litany of Abundant Thanksgiving to God

Let us give thanks to the Lord our God.
It is right to give him thanks and praise.
It is truly fitting and proper, right and profitable, that we should always and everywhere give thanks to You, Lord, Holy Father, almighty and everlasting God.
Lord, have mercy on us.
Christ, have mercy on us.
Lord, have mercy on us. Christ, hear us.
Christ, graciously hear us.

God the Father of heaven, **have mercy on us.**
God the Son, Redeemer of the world, **have mercy on us.**
God the Holy Spirit, **have mercy on us.**
Holy Trinity, one God, **have mercy on us.**

Holy Mary, Mother of God, **lead our song of thanksgiving.**

For light, life and all creation, **we give thanks to you, O God** *(repeat this response after each verse)*:
For the manger, the cross, and the dawn of Easter,
For the dove and the seven flames of heavenly fire,
For the revelation of the mystery of Yourself, the Most Holy Trinity,
For the Queen of Heaven, Your Son's mother and ours,
For the cleansing waters of baptism poured over our heads,
For those who brought us into Your Church,
For father, mother, relatives, and friends,
For homeland, government, and native tongue,
For our daily bread, our home, and our daily work,
For consolation, happiness, and protection in danger,
For the works of penance that You have given us,
For the bitter cup of suffering which makes us strong,

For the anointing of Confirmation which makes us soldiers of the Holy Spirit,
For the sacrifice of Christ's Body and Blood,
For the daily nourishment of this heavenly bread,
For Jesus dwelling among us in the tabernacle,
For healing and strength in the sacrament of reconciliation,
For the consoling oil of the sick, which heals and redeems,
For the power of priests to call upon You,
For the nobility, honor, and dignity of marriage,
For the Church which lifts us up and gathers us together,
For this Rock of Truth withstanding storms and distress,
For Peter, holding the keys of heaven in his hand,
For Your shepherds' royal priesthood,
For religious orders, the fruitful branches on the tree of Your Holy Church,
For the perfect proof of faith,
For the hope of beholding You face to face,
For the privilege of being able to love Your name and glory,
For the assistance of angels in this earthly battle,
For the courage we are given from the merits of the saints,
For all the saints who are interceding for us before Your throne,
For the immaculate purity of the Virgin Mary,
For the Scriptures and the teaching of the *Magisterium*,
For all the glorious victories of Your kingdom,
For all the illustrious feastdays of the Church,
For hearing our intercessions for the dead,
For giving us an immortal soul endowed with intellect,
For ennobling our will with freedom,
For giving us a will for doing good,
For promising eternal rewards for even the smallest of good deeds,
For leading us through life by Your kind providence,
For shining Your light in the darkness of the night,
For letting Your voice be heard even amidst the clouds of disappointment,
For supporting us with Your hand when the ground shakes beneath us,

For the Sacred Heart of Jesus,
For all the graces given us when we deserved only punishment,
For the resurrection of the dead,
For the coming of Christ on the clouds,
For judging the righteous in justice,
For bringing the proud to their knees,
For calling us to our true heavenly homeland,

Lamb of God, You take away the sins of the world,
Spare us, O Lord.
Lamb of God, You take away the sins of the world,
Graciously hear us, O Lord.
Lamb of God, You take away the sins of the world,
Have mercy on us.

Let us pray:
O God, through Your holy Apostle you call us at all times and in all circumstances to give thanks. We humbly beseech You for the grace to begin our thanksgiving here on earth in such a way that we may bring it to perfection in heaven. We ask this through our Lord Jesus Christ, Your Son, Who lives and reigns with You and the Holy Spirit, one God for ever and ever.
Amen.

Chronology of Blessed James' Life

April 5, 1866	Anna Neidl, mother of James, is born in Landegg.
July 6, 1866	Francis Kern, Sr., father of James, is born in Erdberg.
April 11, 1897	James is born "Francis Alexander Kern" in Vienna.
April 19, 1897	James is baptized "Francis Alexander."
Pentecost, 1908	James receives the Sacrament of Confirmation.
September 15, 1908	James enters the Junior Seminary at Hollabrunn.
April 21, 1912	James takes a vow of virginity for life.
October 15, 1915	James reports for military duty with the outbreak of WWI.
January 1, 1916	During the forty hours devotion in the Church of St. Blase in Salzburg, James asks Jesus for the grace to be showered with suffering.
May 15, 1916	James is transferred to the Italian front.
September 10, 1916	James is seriously wounded in battle.
September 13, 1916	James finally reaches a hospital at Folgaria for treatment of his wounds.
October, 1917	James is discharged from the military for medical reasons and returns to the seminary in Vienna.
January, 1918	Isidore Bogdan Zahradnik, a Norbertine priest of Strahov in Prague, apostatizes and works to establish a Czech "national church" after the war.
January 8, 1920	The "Czech National Church" is officially founded.
September 14, 1920	The "Czech National Church" is officially recognized by the state.
October 18, 1920	Francis Kern enters the Norbertine abbey of Geras where he receives his religious name "James."

October 20, 1921	James makes his first profession of vows.
July 11, 1922	James preaches his first sermon as a deacon in the abbey church.
July 23, 1922	James is ordained to the priesthood in St. Stephen's Cathedral, Vienna.
August 1, 1922	James celebrates his first Holy Mass at Vöcklabruck.
Eastertime, 1923	James catches a cold in the confessional that causes him to hemorrhage.
August 10, 1923	James is hospitalized and has four ribs surgically removed.
Christmas, 1923	James convalesces in the Marian hospice at Meran.
July 20, 1924	James preaches his last sermon.
September, 1924	James has four more ribs surgically removed.
October 20, 1924	James renews his vows, receives his last Holy Communion, and dies during surgery.
October 22, 1924	First funeral rite for James is held at Vienna's General Hospital.
October 25, 1924	Solemn funeral rite for James at Geras.
September 26, 1956	James' body is exhumed as an initial step in introducing the beatification process.
September 30, 1956	James' remains are transferred to the abbey church.
November 15, 1956	The petition to introduce James' cause is presented in Rome.
March 18, 1958	The cause for James' beatification is officially opened.
June 21, 1998	James is beatified by Pope John Paul II in Vienna's *Heldenplatz*.

Appendix V:

Bibliography of Blessed James

Promulgatio Decreti super Virtutibus in causa Beatificationis Servi Dei Jacobi Kern, O.Praem. Analecta Praemonstratensia 73 (1997), pp. 136-139.

Documentum in causa Beatificationis Venerabilis Jacobi Kern. Analecta Praemonstratensia 75 (1999), pp. 128-130.

Litterae Abbatis Generalis Hermenegildi J. Noyens omnibus sodalibus Ordinis Praemonstratensis occasione beatificationis Servi Dei Jacobi Kern, Sacerdotis professi Canoniae Gerusenae. Analecta Praemonstratensia 75 (1999), pp. 229-230.

DeBerdt, Olav, O.Praem. *Jakob Franz Kern O.Praem.: Heiligkeitsstreben in unserer Zeit.* Poppe Verlag: 1960.

DeClerck, D.F. *La béatification de Jacob Kern, O.Praem.* Analecta Praemonstratensia 75 (1999), pp. 133-136.

Fleischmann, Kornelius. *Diener Gottes Jakob Kern O.Praem.* Styria: 1984 .

Franz, Isfried. *Geschichte der Waldviertler Klosterstiftung Geras-Pernegg.* Geras: 1947.

Hoekx, E. *Jakob Kern: Norbertijn van de Abdij Geras.* Averbode: 1963.

John Paul II, Pope. "Plant the Cross in your Life!" *(homily given at the beatification of Blessed James).* L'Osservatore Romano (English Edition) n. 25, June 24, 1998.

Schulenburg, Josef. "Jakob Franz Alexander Kern. Ein Beitrag zu einem priesterlichen Lebensbild." *Wiener Kirchenblatt,* January 25/May 3, 1925.

Weidinger, Hermann Josef. *Sühnepriester Jakob Kern.* Graz: 1960.

Weidinger, Hermann Josef. *Jakob Kern - durch Leid sum Licht.* Freunde der Heilkräuter, Karlstein/Thaya: 1999.

For additional copies or information about a vocation in the Norbertine Order please contact:

For MEN (Priests):
Vocation Director
St. Michael's Abbey
19292 El Toro Road
Silverado, CA 92676
TEL (949) 858-0222 x. 333
www.abbeynews.com
E-mail: vocationdirector333@yahoo.com

For WOMEN (Contemplative Nuns):
Mother Prioress
Bethlehem Priory of St. Joseph
17831-A Water Canyon Rd
Tehachapi, CA 93561-7686
TEL (661) 823-1066
E-mail: MotherMaryA@aol.com